ISBN 978-1-5285-9925-2
PIBN 10965475

Forgotten Books is a registered trademark of FB &c Ltd.
Copyright © 2018 FB &c Ltd.
FB &c Ltd, Dalton House, 60 Windsor Avenue, London, SW19 2RR.
Company number 08720141. Registered in England and Wales.

For support please visit www.forgottenbooks.com

English
Français
Deutsche
Italiano
Español
Português

www.forgottenbooks.com

Mythology Photography **Fiction**
Fishing Christianity **Art** Cooking
Essays Buddhism Freemasonry
Medicine **Biology** Music **Ancient**
Egypt Evolution Carpentry Physics
Dance Geology **Mathematics** Fitness
Shakespeare **Folklore** Yoga Marketing
Confidence Immortality Biographies
Poetry **Psychology** Witchcraft
Electronics Chemistry History **Law**
Accounting **Philosophy** Anthropology
Alchemy Drama Quantum Mechanics
Atheism Sexual Health **Ancient History**
Entrepreneurship Languages Sport
Paleontology Needlework Islam
Metaphysics Investment Archaeology
Parenting Statistics Criminology
Motivational

Historic, archived document

Do not assume content reflects current
scientific knowledge, policies, or practices.

RFD LETTER
To
Radio Farm Directors
From
Radio and Television Service
Office of Information – U. S. Department of Agriculture

Special Edition
July 2, 1953

Dear RFD:

   This special letter comes as the announcement that the Department
of Agriculture is initiating, at once, a weekly package service to television stations doing farm service broadcasting as well as land grant colleges.

   As was mentioned in both NARFD "CHATS" and the USDA "RFD Letter"
some time ago, the Department has been conducting a 13 week experimental
package series to determine with what degree of success program materials
can be packaged for television and used to disseminate agricultural information. The response to that series has been most encouraging. The con-
templated service would follow much the same pattern as that series with
a weekly package going to each station or college requesting the service.
Packages would consist of a story (seven minutes or less in length) in
suggested script form complete with the visuals necessary to incorporate
that story into an existing farm program. Visuals such as still pictures,
2X2 slides, artwork, motion film, and live objects would be used.

   In order that this service can be gotten underway at once, it is
proposed that some of the packages distributed during the first 13 weeks
of operation would be duplications of the packages produced in the 13
week TV research series.

   As soon as the topics for the packages to be sent out between now
and September 30 have been approved, those requesting this service will be
sent a listing of them and a schedule to permit integration of this material into station and college program plans.

   If you're doing a weekly or daily farm television show and want
this weekly service of material to incorporate into that show, let us know.
Please send the name of the person to receive the packages and that
person's complete address to us here at Radio and Television Service, USDA,
Washington 25, D. C.

   Incidentally, it is definite that on Friday, July 10, a motion
film package on farm safety, and suitable for use during Farm Safety Week
(July 19 through 25) will be mailed to those requesting the service by that
date.

                Sincerely,

                Ken

                Kenneth M. Gapen
                Ass't Director of Information

                Bob

RFD LETTER
To
Radio Farm Directors
From
Radio and Television Service
Office of Information – U. S. Department of Agriculture

July 3, 1953
Letter No. 567

Dear Radio Farm Director:

Wheat marketing quotas on the 1954 crop have been proclaimed by Secretary Benson. However, wheat farmers will have the opportunity to vote "yes" or "no" on the proposal.

This action by the Secretary is required by law when total wheat supplies reach levels considerably higher than market needs. Right now, the largest wheat supply in our history is shaping up -- exceeding normal supply by half again. Cotton farmers will likely be facing a similar situation this fall.

The purpose of the marketing quotas, and the acreage allotments which would be linked with them, is to limit wheat production next year -- in 1954 -- to bring wheat supplies more nearly in line with our requirements for wheat. Obviously, wheat prices can't be supported indefinitely at 90 percent of parity if total supplies keep climbing still more out of line with wheat needs. The marketing quotas are a step in the direction of halting the build-up of wheat surpluses.

Wheat farmers will have the opportunity to vote on these marketing quotas soon. The exact date will depend on legislation now before Congress which will also clarify other features of the controls.

For the quotas to go into effect, they must be approved by at least two-thirds of the voting wheat farmers. Anything less than two-thirds approval would eliminate the quotas. Secretary Benson is hoping for a large vote. As to the vote itself....he asks only that farmers vote yes or no....just as they think best. He is anxious, though, for all wheat farmers to understand exactly what they will be voting on.

A two-thirds affirmative, or "yes" vote will give wheat farmers price supports at 90 percent of parity on their wheat grown from an allotted acreage. A negative, or "no" vote, by more than a third of the farmers voting, would automatically drop wheat price supports to 50 percent of parity, and farmers would not be under quota controls on their production and marketing. Wheat farmers will be notified of their acreage allotment before the date of the referendum. So, they'll know when they vote how much wheat they could plant under the allotment system.

Massachusetts Listening Survey to be Available Soon

Bill Alford writes from Massachusetts that the radio-television listening survey conducted there several months ago has now gone to press and will soon be ready for distribution to commercial RFD's upon written request. Write to William D. Alford, Extension Editor, University of Massachusetts, Amherst, Mass. Distribution should take place about the last of July or the first of August.

As for Extension distribution, Bill plans to send two copies to each State -- one to the Editor and one to the Radio-TV Editor.

"The main purpose of the survey," Bill writes, "was to poll folks we knew were listening to our programs and to find out first of all what effect television was having on our radio audience, and secondly what time periods our regular listeners prefer for our type of program, both on radio and on television."

A thousand cards went to people requesting material offered on the television program early this year, while an equal number went to radio listeners. The return was an amazing 52 percent.

Bureau of Animal Industry Needs Twin Calves

You RFD's within 300 miles of Washington, D. C., can be of great assistance to the Department in one of its research programs.

The Bureau of Animal Industry would like to know about identical twin calves of any beef or dual-purpose breed. Offers from breeders to sell their twin calves have been very limited this year and as a result the feeding studies at Beltsville may be seriously handicapped. For this reason, the BAI folks have extended from 200 miles to 300 miles the distance they will go to get twin calves.

Breeders within 300 miles of Washington, D. C., who have twin calves of the same sex are requested to write to Dr. C. F. Winchester, Bureau of Animal Industry, Beltsville, Md. Twins 5 months old or younger are desired and they may be Herefords, Shorthorns, Aberdeen Angus, or any cross of these or other beef breeds. Identical twins sired by a beef bull and from a dairy cow may be accepted for experimental use.

Results obtained during the first 4 years of the feeding studies with twin calves showed that those given only enough feed for six months to keep them from losing weight, grew rapidly and economically when they were later placed on adequate rations. The retarded calves required no more total feed to reach a certain weight than was consumed by their co-twins even though the former calves reached the desired weight 2 or 3 months later. Meat of the retarded calves was as good as that from the well-fed co-twins fed as controls. Calves fed on limited calorie rations received adequate allowances of protein, minerals, and Vitamin A. Further information concerning protein requirements of calves on limited rations may be obtained in future feeding studies.

The Drought Week in Review

This was a week of rapid and dramatic action on the drought front.

On Friday -- a week ago today -- Secretary Benson asked President Eisenhower to declare Texas and Oklahoma a major disaster area because of the drought.

On Saturday and Sunday the Secretary visited the drought area in Texas and observed the situation first-hand. While on tour, the Secretary announced that a request had been filed with the Interstate Commerce Commission to permit railroads to reduce rates for emergency drought movements.

On Tuesday the President designated 152 Texas counties and 40 Oklahoma counties as a "major disaster area" and authorized $8 million from his emergency fund to get a relief program under way.

On the same day several railroads serving the Southwest moved to back up the emergency relief measures. They announced they were planning to lower freight rates on feed moving into the area, and that they were also making a special effort to have cars available when and where needed.

The Department also announced on Tuesday that it would step up its beef purchase program to provide at least 200 million pounds of canned beef, gravy, hamburger and boned beef for next year's school lunch program and other outlets.

On Wednesday the President added parts of Kansas, Colorado, Arkansas, and New Mexico to the designated disaster area.

On Thursday the Department announced that supplies of feed concentrates and grain from Commodity Credit Corporation stocks will be made available to eligible farmers and ranchers in the emergency drought areas under a schedule of reduced prices.

State committees are being established in each of the disaster states and local committees in each drought county to consider applications and establish eligibility for feed and emergency credit. Federal credit agencies are taking such action as they can within present limits of authorities and funds and Congress is considering proposals for a loan program more specifically adapted to the emergency needs.

Market Improvement in Southwest

We mentioned last week the increase in cattle receipts at the Southwestern markets as a result of the drought. It was a different situation this week -- at Fort Worth, Oklahoma City, Wichita, San Antonio and Kansas City. Receipts were 30 percent less than last week. Anticipation of a definite relief program, and rain in some areas, were factors in withholding cattle from the market. The full price advance for the week was $1.00 to $2.00. Apparently cattle buyers in other sections moved into the Southwest as a result of market reports showing the bargain prices prevailing last week. Stocker buyers competed with killers for young thin cows and a few loads of cows with calves at side sold for shipment north.

TV Workshop Report Available from Cornell

We were very happy to receive from Bill Ward copies of the case history report of the recent television workshops arranged by Cornell and carried out by WBEN-TV Buffalo, WHEN Syracuse, and WRGB Schenectady. Bill says he'll be glad to send copies to RFD's and TFD's who request them. Write William B. Ward, Head, Department of Extension Teaching and Information, Cornell University, Ithaca, N. Y.

The report reviews the experiences -- the successes and failures -- of planning and presenting three television workshops for Extension workers. It was published as an aid for those who plan to organize similar workshops in the future. It's full of good ideas.

More than 250 county agents and specialists attended the three workshops, and applications had to be turned down for the Buffalo workshop. Bill says they've had a number of requests for a similar workshop in the New York City area.

Network Farm and Home Shows July 11

NBC National Farm and Home Hour...Saturday 1:00 to 1:30 p.m. EDT. "USDA Headlines" from Washington. Subject of the feature will be the July Crop Report, with Sterling R. Newell and Charles E. Burkhead of the Crop Reporting Board, and Bob Crom.

ABC American Farmer....Saturday 12:30 to 1:00 p.m. EDT. "Top of the Farm News" from Washington. The feature will be "What the Futures Markets Mean to Farmers," with J. M. Mehl, Director of the Commodities Exchange Authority, and Jack Towers.

CBS Radio Farm News...Saturday 3:30 to 3:45 p.m. EDT with Claude Mahoney.

Cordially,

Ken and Don

Ken Gapen and Don Looper
Radio and Television Service

Enclosure
The Grain Storage Situation
and Needs

RFD LETTER
To
Radio Form Directors
From
Radio and Television Service
Office of Information – U. S. Department of Agriculture

July 10, 1953
Letter No. 568

Dear Radio Farm Director:

Watch for Secretary Benson's announcement of the national wheat acreage allotment by next Wednesday (July 15). That's the deadline provided by law.

As this is written, Congressional action is still pending on legislation affecting wheat quotas and acreage allotments. This may change the total allotment, the eligibility to vote, and the latest date on which the referendum can be held.

Unless that date is changed, the referendum will be held not later than July 24 as required by the present law.

Third Largest Crop Production in Prospect

The third largest crop production of record is in prospect this year, according to the July 1 Crop Report issued today.

The near-record production of spring wheat in prospect and the above average winter wheat crop being harvested, amount to a larger than average all wheat total of 1,175 million bushels. The corn crop of over 3.3 billion bushels in prospect would be the second largest of record.

The severe drought in the central and southern Great Plains, while causing heavy acreage loss of crops, is causing greatest concern at present in connection with pastures and livestock.

The total volume of all crops this year is expected to be about 30 percent above the 1923-32 average. If realized, this would be exceeded only by the record 1948 production and the near-record 1952 total. The acreage of crops to be harvested this year is only about average, but high yields are expected for several major crops. For a large number of major crops, production will be relatively large, but none is expected to set a new record.

Foot and Mouth Disease Situation

We're mailing you tonight a release on the progress of the foot and mouth disease eradication program in Mexico. JUL 3 1 1953

Cricket Outbreak Halted in West

The biggest outbreak of Mormon crickets since 1940 has been halted in the West. These crop and range land pests have been controlled on nearly a half million acres in five states, thus providing protection for millions of adjacent acres. Poisoned bait was distributed in Nevada, California, Utah, Idaho, and Colorado under a program carried out cooperatively by the Department of Agriculture, Federal land-managing agencies, State, county, and local agencies.

Except for limited mopping-up work, the control work is completed for this year. This year's control has prevented crop damage, stopped migrations, and has delayed, if not prevented, a major Mormon cricket outbreak in future years. Outbreaks sometimes continue for several years unless checked.

Under Secretary Heads Delegation to Sugar Conference

Under Secretary of Agriculture True D. Morse has been named by President Eisenhower to serve as delegate and chairman of the U. S. Delegation to the International Sugar Conference in London beginning July 13. Lawrence Myers, director of PMA's Sugar Branch, is alternate.

The conference will deal with world sugar surpluses and will undertake negotiations toward drawing up a new International Sugar Agreement to replace the Agreement of 1937 which has largely been in abeyance since the start of World War II. Secretary Benson says, "It is our hope that a new International Sugar Agreement can be an effective means of reducing or eliminating direct and indirect export subsidies on sugar."

Cotton Acreage Report

The Crop Reporting Board this week estimated cotton in cultivation July 1, 1953, at 24,618,000 acres -- 9 percent less than a year earlier but 12 percent more than the 10-year average.

The Board said, however, that this estimate may include about $1\frac{1}{2}$ million acres of cotton that has been planted but is not up. Many growers considered this to be cotton acreage in cultivation and included it in their July 1 reports. Most of this acreage is in northwest Texas and in Arkansas.

Calling to Your Attention...

We have a few copies of the statement by R. I. Farrington, Acting Director, Agricultural Credit Services, on H.R. 6054, before the House Committee on Agriculture Monday, July 6. H.R. 6054 is the bill introduced July 1 to provide for additional emergency assistance to farmers and stockmen. A companion bill was introduced in the Senate the same day by Senator Aiken and 52 other Senators. Write us if you want Mr. Farrington's statement.

We mailed you on Monday a statement by Secretary Benson advising farmers and cattlemen to review the cattle outlook before rushing cattle to market. We mailed you today for release Monday, July 13, a good story about a better method of planting grass and clover seed -- through precision placement of both seed and fertilizer.

Farm Safety Week Luncheon

Vice President Richard M. Nixon, Assistant Secretary of Agriculture J. Earl Coke, and Ned H. Dearborn, president of the National Safety Council, will be the principal speakers at a luncheon to launch the 10th observance of National Farm Safety Week on July 18.

The luncheon will be held in the Chinese Room of the Mayflower Hotel here in Washington. The program for the luncheon will be broadcast on "The American Farmer" program over the American Broadcasting Company network from 12:30 - 1:00 p.m. EDT. More than 100 distinguished farm and safety leaders are expected to attend.

Vice President Nixon is expected to re-emphasize the purpose of National Farm Safety Week by stressing the humanitarian nature of the war on accidents to people who farm to live. He will dedicate his remarks to the relatives of the 14,000 farm residents killed in accidents in 1952.

Mr. Coke and Mr. Dearborn will join in asking all farm and safety leaders to take an active part in the 10th observance of the Week, and Mr. Dearborn is expected to make a special appeal to ministers to discuss the Commandment "Thou Shall Not Kill", as the humanitarian theme of the first day of National Farm Safety Week. The theme of the week, taken from the President's proclamation, is "Farm to Live and Live to Farm".

2 New Peach Varieties Announced

The Department this week announced two new peach varieties for the South -- Coronet and Maygold. Both were developed at the U. S. Horticultural Field Laboratory at Fort Valley, Ga.

Coronet has been tested at State agricultural experiment stations in most of the southern States and in commercial orchards in Georgia. It is recommended for trial planting to replace the commercial variety Dixigem. Compared with Dixigem, the fruit of Coronet is firmer, more highly colored, and slightly earlier in ripening.

Maygold is an early variety for the Deep South. It is recommended for planting in southern locations where December and January are warm months but temperatures averaging 54 degrees Fahrenheit may be expected. The new peach -- a yellow clingstone -- ripens in May.

2 New Bermuda Grass Hybrids Developed

Two new Bermuda grass hybrids -- Suwannee for pastures and Tiffine for turf -- are announced by the Department and the Georgia Coastal Plain Experiment Station. They were developed in Federal-State research at Tifton, Ga.

Suwannee does well on deep sand and has an outstanding ability to make use of nitrogen applied as fertilizer. It will be released in small quantities to certified growers this summer, and sprigs should be available for general farm planting within the coming year.

New Crop Insurance Film Available for TV

You TV-RFD's may be interested in a new 15-minute black and white film recently released by the Federal Crop Insurance Corporation. Titled "The Big Gamble", the film contains many dramatic sequences showing the farmers' struggle with Nature to produce a crop. The film is fully cleared for TV showing and is available in both 16 mm. and 35 mm. sizes.

The film is recommended for showing in areas where crop insurance is available. Because of its length, it is perhaps best used on a half-hour show, which allows time for local crop insurance officials to appear and discuss local or regional aspects of the crop insurance program.

Films are obtainable from State Crop Insurance Directors. A listing of names and addresses of directors follows (look for your State):

Dewey H. McCollough, Old Post Office Building, Rm. 404-5-6-7-8, Montgomery 4, Alabama; C. S. Dupree, P. O. Box 2781, Little Rock, Arkansas; Wesley Schlotzhauer, 1515 Clay Street, Room 701, Oakland 12, California; Burrell J. Monroe, 948 Broadway, Denver 3, Colorado.

William R. Huey, Old Post Office Bldg., Athens, Georgia; John P. Mix, P. O. Box 4068, Boise, Idaho; John W. Hodge, Room 201, U. S. Post Office and Courthouse, Springfield, Illinois; Lenard C. Pound, Agriculture Bldg., Room 304, 215 E. New York St., Indianapolis 4, Indiana; Alvin J. Cook, Iowa Building, 505 6th Ave., Des Moines 9, Iowa.

Dean W. Bernitz, 1122 Moro Street, Manhattan, Kansas; O. R. Wheeler, Mill and Maxwell Sts., Lexington 29, Kentucky; Charles H. Evans, 1517 6th Street, Alexandria, Louisiana; Harry K. Fox, P. O. Box 1200, Lansing 4, Michigan; Elmer Tabor, P. O. Box 3110, St. Paul, Minnesota; James S. Smith, Room 304-305 Masonic Temple Building, 1130 W. Capitol St., Jackson 3, Mississippi; George L. Carlton, IOOF Bldg., 10th and Walnut Sts., Columbia, Missouri; Henry L. Anderson, Box 519, Lewistown, Montana.

L. Ralph Robertson, P. O. Box 31, Lincoln 1, Nebraska; Joe L. Matthews, P. O. Box 362, Albuquerque, New Mexico; Lynn L. Watson, Byrne Bldg., 236 W. Genesee St., Syracuse 2, New York; Julian E. Mann, 216-19 PMA Bldg., State College Campus, Raleigh, North Carolina; P. J. Kettwig, P. O. Box 2017, Fargo, North Dakota.

Edgar F. Hempy, Rm. 224 Old Federal Bldg., Third and State Sts., Columbus 15, Ohio; George E. Dysinger, Etherton Bldg., 6th and Main Sts., Stillwater, Oklahoma; Willis B. Bergey, 928 N. Third St., Harrisburg, Pennsylvania; E. M. Derham, P. O. Box 660, Columbia 1, South Carolina; James P. Paulsen, P. O. Box 843, Huron, South Dakota.

J. Bruce Joyner, U. S. Courthouse, Room 510, Nashville 3, Tennessee; O. B. Briggs, PMA Bldg., College Station, Texas; J. Beverly Farrar, 609 E. Main Street, Richmond 19, Virginia; Murl E. Cummings, 206 Hutton Bldg., Spokane, Washington.

Sydney B. Huseby, 3010 Washington Ave., Madison, Wisconsin; Curtis Hicks, P. O. Box 1211, 345 E. 2nd St., Casper, Wyoming; J. Francis Buck, Br. Mgr., 623 South Wabash Ave., Chicago 5, Illinois (Chicago Branch Office); and C. D. Laidlaw, Federal Crop Insurance Corporation, USDA, South Bldg., Washington 25, D. C.

Arizona is served by California, Connecticut by New York, Delaware by Pennsylvania, Maryland by Pennsylvania, Massachusetts by New York, Nevada by California, New Jersey and West Virginia by Pennsylvania, Oregon by Washington, and Utah by Idaho.

Network Farm and Home Shows July 18

NBC National Farm and Home Hour...Saturday originating at 1:00 to 1:30 p.m. EDT. "USDA Headlines" from Washington. A Farm Safety Week feature with Homer Martz of KDKA and Bill Givens of KYW.

ABC American Farmer...Saturday originating at 12:30 to 1:00 p.m. EDT. "Top of the Farm News" from USDA. The feature will be a pickup from the National Farm Safety Week luncheon in Washington with Vice President Nixon, Assistant Secretary of Agriculture Coke, and Ned H. Dearborn, President of the National Safety Council.

CBS Radio Farm News...Saturday originating 3:30 to 3:45 p.m. EDT with Claude Mahoney.

Among Ourselves...

Ken Gapen is off to Berkeley for the annual meeting of the American Association of Agricultural College Editors. He'll be contacting a few of you RFD's between here and there.

Lyle Webster, Director of the Office of Information, will also be attending the AAACE meeting, July 13-15, as will several other Department representatives.

Word comes from Oklahoma that Max Kirkland, who has been Extension RFD at Oklahoma A. and M., has moved to New Jersey to replace Clem Lewis on Sam Reck's staff. We reported several weeks ago that Clem was leaving Rutgers to become show manager for the New Jersey Mid-Atlantic Farm Show.

The Foreign Agriculture folks tell us that the Mutual Security Agency folks are very happy about the results of the European RFD's visit to the United States, and most enthusiastic about the contribution of the RFD group in this country.

Cordially,

Don

Don Looper
Radio and Television Service

Enclosure
Report of Developments on
Eradication of VE

RFD LETTER
To
Radio Farm Directors
From
Radio and Television Service
Office of Information – U. S. Department of Agriculture

July 17, 1953
Letter No. 569

Dear Radio Farm Director:

Friday, August 14, is the day wheat farmers will vote for or against marketing quotas for the 1954 crop. Secretary Benson set the date this week at the same time he announced a national acreage allotment of 62 million acres for the 1954 wheat crop.

The announcement followed Congressional action which established a new minimum national allotment figure, and provided authorization to hold the referendum as late as mid-August. Under these new provisions, the national allotment for 1954 may not be less than 62 million acres. Since the indicated 1953-54 wheat supply stands at an all-time high, the minimum acreage -- 62 million -- is called for. Under the previous legislation, the national allotment for 1954 would have been only 55 million acres. (The 1953 planted acreage was 78.6 million.)

The national acreage allotment is apportioned among the states, the state allotments among the counties, and the county allotments among individual farms. In general, all farms which grew wheat in any one of the years 1951, 1952 or 1953 will be assigned an acreage allotment. Then, if marketing quotas are approved, the individual farm marketing quota is the wheat actually produced on the allotted acres.

Wheat quotas were proclaimed by the Secretary on July 1. But they will not become effective unless approved by at least two-thirds of the growers voting in the August 14 referendum. Growers with more than 15 acres planted to wheat, and with normal production of 200 bushels or more, are subject to the quotas and are therefore eligible to vote.

Here in brief are the issues at stake in the August 14 referendum:

IF THE VOTE IS YES --

1. Marketing quotas will be in effect for all farms planting more than 15 acres of wheat.

2. Marketing penalties will apply on any wheat produced on acres in excess of the farm's allotment.

3. Price support at 90 percent of parity will be available for those who stay within their acreage allotment.

4. Quotas can be expected to hold down production, helping to bring supplies more nearly in line with the effective market demand.

IF THE VOTE IS NO --

1. There will be no marketing quotas, with their penalty controls.

2. Acreage allotments, however, will continue in effect.

3. Price supports will drop to 50 percent of parity for coopera-
tors. Non-cooperators -- any who exceed their acreage allotments -- will
not be entitled to price support, even at the 50 percent level.

4. In the absence of quota controls, production can be expected
to continue at higher levels -- possibly adding to the wheat surplus.

Nominations Confirmed for Assistant Secretaries

The Senate on Thursday confirmed Presidential nominations of John
H. Davis and Romeo E. Short, each to be an Assistant Secretary of Agriculture.
These positions were provided in Reorganization Plan No. 2 of 1953, passed
early in June by the Congress.

The plan also provided for an Administrative Assistant Secretary
to be under the classified civil service system. Richard D. Aplin has been
appointed to that position by Secretary of Agriculture Ezra Taft Benson with
the approval of the President.

Mr. Davis has been serving under Secretary Benson as President
of the Commodity Credit Corporation and Director, Commodity Marketing and
Adjustment. Since January Mr. Short has served in the Department, first
as Director, Agricultural Credit Services, and since early March as
Director of the Foreign Agricultural Service. Mr. Aplin has been Director
of Departmental Administration.

C. R. Arnold is New Governor of FCA

The Senate on Thursday confirmed President Eisenhower's appoint-
ment of C. R. (Cap) Arnold of Hilliards, Ohio, as governor of the Farm
Credit Administration to complete the unexpired term of I. W. Duggan who
resigned last month.

Mr. Arnold retired in 1950 after 10 years as production credit
commissioner of FCA. Before that he was deputy commissioner, after having
come to the Farm Credit Administration as special assistant to the governor
when it was first established in 1933. He has spent the last 2 years on
his 350-acre livestock and crop farm.

Flagging to Your Attention

We mailed you the full text of Secretary Benson's Fresno speech.
We've also briefed it for attachment to this Letter. Also mailed to you
were the wheat quota announcement, a release on the new credit legislation,
and a good VE situationer.

New Disaster Credit Legislation

The new disaster credit legislation passed by Congress and approved by the President this week does three principal things: (1) It provides a supplemental source of credit for farmers in the disaster areas. (2) It makes it easier to administer feed and seed and other assistance programs in the disaster areas. (3) It sets up special credit machinery for livestock operators whether in the disaster areas or not.

Here are the main provisions:

1. Economic disaster loans. This provides a supplemental source of emergency credit for established farmers in areas designated by the President as major disaster areas. When the Secretary of Agriculture finds that farmers in these areas have felt the force of an economic disaster -- such as a substantial price decline -- to the extent they cannot get needed credit from local sources to carry on farming operations, he can authorize loans to meet that need. These emergency loans will be similar to the disaster loans now being made by the Farmers Home Administration to farmers who have suffered production losses from natural disasters such as drought, flood and windstorm.

2. Emergency assistance in furnishing feed and seed. This provides that in the future whatever expense the Government bears in supplying feed and seed in disaster areas will be borne by a disaster loan revolving fund under the jurisdiction of the Secretary of Agriculture. In the past this expense had been carried by the President's emergency fund.

3. Special livestock loans. This provides emergency loans to farmers and cattlemen who need Federal credit to buy feed and pay operating expenses. Heaviest demand is expected from the drought-stricken southwest, but these loans are not limited to the disaster area.

This credit will be extended only to established producers and feeders of cattle, sheep and goats, who have a reasonable chance of working out of their difficulties but cannot obtain the funds they need from private or cooperative credit sources. Loans will be made in amounts of $2,500 and more, at 5 percent interest for periods up to 3 years. They can be renewed if renewal is found to be in the best interest of the farmer and the Government. All applications will be passed on by special livestock loan committees to be appointed by Secretary Benson.

Network Farm and Home Shows July 25

NBC National Farm and Home Hour...Saturday originating at 1:00 to 1:30 p.m. EDT. "USDA Headlines" from Washington. Feature from the annual meeting in Toronto of the American Veterinary Medical Association to report progress being made in controlling various livestock diseases.

ABC American Farmer...Saturday originating at 12:30 to 1:00 p.m. EDT. "Top of the Farm News" from USDA. There will be a feature from Washington on the wheat acreage allotments and marketing quotas.

CBS Radio Farm News...Saturday originating 3:30 to 3:45 p.m. EDT with Claude Mahoney.

Cattle Market Sharply Higher

That was some cattle market we had this week. Here's a brief review:

Reduced marketings of fed cattle continued through the first three days this week and prices were sharply higher each day. The price peak was reached on Wednesday when Choice and Prime steers sold $2.50 to $6.00 higher than last week. Excessively large receipts Thursday resulted in declines of $1 to $2, leaving a net advance for the week of $1.50 to $4.50 on Choice and Prime steers.

At most markets cows sold 50 cents to $1 higher at the close, and grass slaughter steers $2 to $3 higher. Marketings of cows, calves, and yearlings in the southwest drought area were only moderate and prices advanced another 50 cents to $1 in a very active trade. All cattle and calves at the close of the week were selling $1.50 to $4 higher than the low time three weeks ago.

All-Out Beef Campaign Postponed

As a result of higher cattle and beef prices during the past week, the meat industry is postponing the all-out "eat more beef" campaign which was scheduled to begin August 1. Industry and the Department of Agriculture are still planning to push retail beef sales during August and September, but not with the all-out campaign originally planned.

Assistant Secretary of Agriculture John H. Davis wired the following to industry representatives on Thursday:

"Increased supplies of grass cattle are still in prospect for the next several months and a further step-up in consumption of beef, particularly from the lower grades of cattle, continues a highly desirable objective. While a sustained merchandising program in this direction is still as necessary for the summer and fall period as appeared when we last met, we believe that some delay in the start of the industry's full-scale promotion and in the inauguration of the very extensive campaigns planned by individual organizations, would be appropriate and more effective than a firm August 1 target."

Cattle Report Reflects Heavy Marketings

The July 1 cattle-on-feed report, issued this week, reflects the heavy marketings that have taken place this year. On July 1, the number of cattle on feed in the Corn Belt was only 8 percent greater than on the same date last year. On April 1 the increase had been 19 percent above a year earlier and on January 1, 23 percent above a year earlier. Feedlots have been emptied faster than last year and they have generally not been refilled quite as fast.

In the eastern Corn Belt, the number of cattle on feed July 1 was 5 percent larger than last year, while the western Corn Belt showed an increase of 10 percent. Strictly short term feeding is at the lowest level in several seasons. Only 2 percent of the fed cattle marketed between April 1 and July 1 had been placed on feed after April 1.

Considering information available on several important states outside the Corn Belt, it appears that the number of cattle on feed July 1 for the country as a whole was up 4 to 5 percent from July 1 a year ago, compared with an increase of 16 percent on January 1 and a 12 to 14 percent increase on April 1.

Eligibility for Drought Feed Clarified

The basis of farmer and stockman eligibility for Government-owned feeds being made available in southwestern drought areas was clarified by the Department Thursday in a telegram to chairmen of drought committees in Texas, Oklahoma, New Mexico, Colorado, and Kansas.

For the purpose of the drought feed program, the Department defined foundation herds as consisting of cows, bulls, nursing calves and heifers that are needed to replace over-age and other undesirable cattle culled from herds.

More specifically, to be eligible for feed at reduced prices, a farmer or stockman must, first, have less than a 30-day supply of feed to supplement roughage to maintain his foundation herd. Such feed, however, may be fed to cattle other than those in the foundation herd if they are to be marketed not later than September 30, 1953, and provided they are not feeders in feed lots; and second, farmers and ranchers must not have the financial ability to remain in business and satisfactorily maintain their herds unless they can purchase feed at prices substantially below the prevailing market price.

Toward a New Foreign Trade Policy

Director R. E. Short of the Foreign Agricultural Service said Thursday that "Our greatest assurance against regimentation of American agriculture lies in finding a solution to our trade problems."

Speaking before the General Assembly of Farm and Home Week at Mississippi State College, Mr. Short said, "The root of our problem is that the United States needs a new, realistic foreign trade policy, one that accelerates trade rather than restricts it...

"It is our hope and our goal that during this next year we can modify, we can clarify, we can improve the foreign trade policies that affect our agricultural exports. While these greater policies are being shaped we do not intend to take precipitous action that later we may regret - such as dumping our agricultural surpluses abroad with no regard for the economic effect upon other friendly nations."

But Mr. Short added that our Government is going ahead with interim actions to help the situation, such as these:

1. The President has been successful in obtaining approval for extending the Reciprocal Trade Agreements Act for another year, thus keeping alive the only trade expansion program that we currently have.

2. Progress is being made on simplifying our customs procedures, which too often have been barriers to useful goods.

3. The Congress is considering ways and means of making our surplus commodities available to needy countries, both to meet emergencies and as part of our aid program.

4. We are helping a great number of other countries to improve their economies, and thereby their purchasing power, by giving them technical assistance.

5. We are sending out an increasing number of commodity specialists to do on-the-spot reporting of market opportunities abroad.

6. FAS is continuing its function of keeping American agriculture supplied with current information on world trade and commodity developments.

Cordially,

Don

Don Looper
Radio and Television Service

Enclosures:
Beef Fact Sheet
Ants in the Home and Garden
US-FAO News Letter

ATTACHMENT

Excerpts from "Charting the Course," Address by Secretary Benson before the
Agricultural Council of California, the California Farm Bureau Federation,
the California State Grange, the California State Chamber of Commerce, and
the California State Board of Agriculture, Fresno, Calif., July 16, 1953.

Despite the difficulties many farmers are encountering in the Nation --
such difficulties as drought in some areas and floods in others, feed
shortages in one place and surplus in another -- our agriculture is firmly
and solidly based. It will go on to surmount these and whatever other
problems may arise.

We have acted swiftly to help alleviate the distress caused by this drought.
President Eisenhower did not become Chief Executive of this country and I
did not become Secretary of Agriculture to stand idly by while farmers go
through the wringer of economic distress, whether due to drought or some
other cause.

I have said many times that I feel our present rigid price support programs
must be improved. They do not build markets, they invite the competition
of substitute products, and they hamper needed production adjustments. The
American people developed farm programs to help farmers pull out of de-
pression. They made changes in the programs to help the economy fight a
war. Now we need to develop further improvements to enable farmers to
achieve stability, prosperity, and parity of living under present day conditions.

The approach is on three fronts.

First, we are going to the grassroots. I have written to the leaders of the
general farm organizations, asking them to have their members debate the
issues. All of the major organizations -- the Farm Bureau, the Grange and
the Farmers Union -- have responded with enthusiasm.

A second avenue of approach is being taken by the Congress. The House
Committee on Agriculture, headed by Congressman Clifford Hope, will hold
hearings throughout the length and breadth of agricultural America. They
will listen to farmers' opinions, evaluate them and weigh them in the light
of experience.

The third approach is being carried on by the Department of Agriculture...
We have made specific requests for the study of certain problems of farm
price support legislation. I wrote more than 60 personal letters to farm
leaders at the agricultural colleges, to directors of research institutions,
and to other leaders in farming affairs . . . We have had excellent re-
sponses to these letters. They have been summarized, and are being further
explored.

In spite of the fact that I am not now ready to make positive recommendations, I do believe that the people are entitled to know the judgments of
our best professional men. Therefore I wish to bring to you, for your
information but without my endorsement, the major suggestions that were
made in reply to my requests.

These are the major objectives of agricultural price policy as set forth
by those who responded to our inquiry:

1. The objective of full parity prices and income for farm people can be
achieved only with a steady level of prices, high employment and production,
and rising output per worker in our total national economy.

2. Equality of economic opportunity is a basic right of agriculture.
Government has a responsibility for maintaining and widening the channels
through which such equality may be attained. The small size of the typical
farming unit and the limited bargaining power of farmers make agriculture
a proper object of public assistance in research, education, and marketing.

3. Agricultural resources should be used effectively. The destruction of
food, the holding idle of productive agricultural resources and a prolonged
delay in the adjustment to new technology -- these are obstacles to the
efficient use of resources which the public will not tolerate indefinitely.

4. Farmers should be protected against the price swings of the free market.
It is generally agreed that the wilder fluctuations of the free market do
not serve a useful economic purpose. Farmers are particularly exposed to
the effects of these fluctuations, and need protection against them.

In appraising our past experience and making recommendations for the future,
some of the best students of agriculture in the Nation reached the following
conclusions:

It was generally agreed that our present agricultural program is heading
for serious trouble and is in need of major overhauling.

Next, with the exception of tobacco and possibly of cotton, it was
generally thought that restricted production was not the answer. Nevertheless, the necessity of production control was clearly indicated if price
support at a rigid high level is to be maintained.

For several of our major export crops, including wheat, it was felt that
two-price plans and multiple-price plans deserved consideration. Such
plans are intended to give substantial price support to that quantity of
a product sold in the domestic market, and to permit sale of additional
quantities to secondary outlets or on the world market at competitive prices.

Recommendations were that farm programs be tailored to the needs of each
specific product rather than forcing all commodities into the same type of
program. The use of modernized parity was recommended, with transitional
parity to help make the change. Thus support prices would reflect current
conditions of demand and cost. Finally, the principle of flexibility was
generally but not unanimously preferred over the present system of rigid
high supports.

The judgments that come from our three-pronged inquiry, and the recommendations that the Department of Agriculture will ultimately make to the Congress,
certainly will not suit everyone ... But I am sure that we can find enough
common ground among these different views on which to build a sound farm
program.

RFD LETTER
To
Radio Form Directors
From
Radio and Television Service
Office of Information – U. S. Department of Agriculture

AUG 3 1953

July 24, 1953
Letter No. 570

Dear Radio Farm Director:

The Department is making use of all its field offices and all other available means of communication to give farmers information on the wheat marketing quota referendum. Information materials have already gone to state and county offices of Department agencies, and we hope that by August 14 every eligible farmer will understand what the referendum means to him.

We're not telling farmers how to vote, but rather telling them what the issues are, and encouraging them to vote their convictions. Regardless of the individual wheat farmer's point of view, the results of the wheat quota referendum on August 14 will directly influence his farming operations during the coming season.

We know that the RFD's will turn in their usual good job of keeping their farm listeners informed. We're enclosing copies of two information materials which we think will be of most use to you -- a Wheat Quota Referendum leaflet and Wheat Marketing Quotas Questions and Answers. We'll also be sending you, today or the first of next week, the announcement of wheat acreage allotments by states.

Mixed Feed Available in Drought Program

Farmers and ranchers eligible for emergency feed aid in designated drought disaster areas may now purchase mixed feed at a reduced price.

The Commodity Credit Corporation have been selling corn, wheat, oats, and cottonseed meal or pellets at below-market prices to enable livestock producers to maintain their basic herds. Now, farmers and ranchers certified by the local committee for participation in the program will have a choice of the feeds already announced as available, or of a mixed feed containing 40 percent corn and 40 percent cottonseed meal.

The mixed feed will be made available by feed mixers or distributors at prices that will reflect the prices at which CCC will make the corn and cottonseed meal available to them.

Watch for...

The lamb crop report next Thursday, agricultural prices Friday.

Speaking of Drought...

Two RFD's who have been all over the drought counties of southeast Colorado think that some stories of "dust bowl" conditions in that area have been exaggerated. There's a serious problem there all right, but there isn't a dust bowl situation, they say. There's little more blowing than usual at this time of year.

But it's dry. And cattlemen whose pastures were almost burned up are faced with serious decisions. The grass is still alive, and rains could bring it back to provide feed for the rest of summer and fall. But without rains there'll be no range feed.

So the alternatives are these: On the one hand, the cattleman can market stock that isn't in market condition and get lower prices for it... and not be in a position to take advantage of possible later rains. Or he can hold on to his stock and pray for rain to enable him to carry it...and to pay off the mortgage.

Citrus Marketing Specialist to Europe

The Department of Agriculture is sending a marketing specialist to the citrus markets of Europe under its program of expanding foreign markets and trade opportunities for United States citrus fruits and citrus products.

The specialist, J. Henry Burke, will visit the citrus markets of the United Kingdom, France, Belgium, the Netherlands, Western Germany, Switzerland, Norway, Sweden and Denmark, and the producing areas of Spain and Italy.

New CCC Advisory Board to Meet August 6-7

The Commodity Credit Corporation's new Advisory Board, appointed by President Eisenhower on July 16, will hold its first meeting on August 6 and 7, Secretary Benson announced today.

The new members are Rudolph K. Froker, Dean, Wisconsin College of Agriculture, Madison, Wis.; Theodore Funk, Treasurer, Funk Bros. Seed Co., Bloomington, Ill.; Arnold William Groth, Vice President, National Bank of Portland, Portland, Oreg.; Herbert J. Hughes, Vice President, National Association of Wheat Growers, Imperial, Neb.; and William Rhea Blake, Executive Vice-president, National Cotton Council, Memphis, Tenn.

The function of the Advisory Board is to study and advise the Secretary with respect to the general policies of the Corporation, including its policies in connection with the purchase, storage, and sale of commodities, and the operation of lending and price support programs. The Act also requires that the Board have bi-partisan membership and shall meet at the call of the Secretary at least once every 90 days.

Flagging to Your Attention...

We mailed you today an address to be delivered by Ass't Secretary John H. Davis before the 34th Annual Conference for Teachers of Vocational Agriculture, Michigan State College, next Tuesday, July 28. You'll also receive the announcement of a new USDA plan for seed stock disposal.

New Advisory Commission Established

An 18-man bi-partisan National Agricultural Advisory Commission was established this week by President Eisenhower. It replaces a 14-man interim advisory agricultural committee which has been serving the Secretary of Agriculture in an advisory capacity since last December.

The President will appoint the members and designate the chairman. Not more than nine can be members of any one political party and at least 12 of them must be representative farmers. The commission will meet at least quarterly, at the request of the Secretary.

It will review national agricultural policies and the administration of farm programs and make recommendations to the Secretary for the improvement of these policies and programs.

Butter Sales to the Army

The Department announced this week that an additional 3,803,115 pounds of butter are being turned over to the Department of the Army under an arrangement to supply the Army with butter acquired under price support operations at prices competitive with other spreads.

This brings butter sales to the Army to 5,770,336 pounds since the initial sale on June 10. Present indications are that approximately nine million additional pounds of butter will be turned over to the Army during the next month.

USDA Meat Purchases

The Department also announced that purchase of two beef products for the week of July 20 totaled 2,938,000 pounds. They include 1,960,000 pounds of canned beef and 978,000 pounds of hamburger. The USDA will continue to accept offers next week for canned beef and hamburger, being purchased with Section 32 funds.

Purchases of frozen carcass beef for export to Greece under an MSA purchase program will resume after the first of August. No purchases of mutton under an MSA requisition for Greece were made this week -- prices quoted were still higher than could be justified.

Network Farm and Home Shows August 1

NBC National Farm and Home Hour...Saturday originating at 1:00 to 1:30 p.m. EDT. "USDA Headlines" from Washington with a special story on wheat quotas.

ABC American Farmer...Saturday originating at 12:30 to 1:00 p.m. EDT. "Top of the Farm News" from USDA. The feature will be "IFYE Visitors Make a Report", a pickup from Kansas City with Bruce Davies KCMO, and a group of Indian exchange delegates.

CBS Radio Farm News...Saturday originating 3:30 to 3:45 p.m. EDT with Claude Mahoney.

Among Ourselves

　　　　Here's a note on the American Association of Agricultural College Editors annual meeting at the University of California at Berkeley, as Ken saw it:

　　　　NARFD Prexie Mal Hansen, Henry Schacht of KNBC, Hamilton Hintz of McClatchy radio, and I, along with a number of state extension radio-TV people, were among the nearly 200 persons attending (about 125 actual information people.)

　　　　Henry Schacht was on the program to outline what he wants as a commercial station farm broadcaster. Ham Hintz suggested ways of making extension agents more effective broadcasters. The radio-TV sessions were geared to extension needs, of course, and services to RFD's were reported by most states. A county extension TV series was demonstrated ably by two agents at KPIX San Francisco.

　　　　On the way out I talked to Gus Swanson KFEL, Don Peach KOA, and Lowell Watts KLZ. Lowell had been back from the Azores about a month when I was in Denver. Carl Herzman, who handled the job while Lowell was away, likely will turn to TV and Lowell will center efforts on radio. However, plans and personalities indicate that it'll be a well knit team job. Carl was on vacation while I was there.

　　　　At Berkeley, I saw Bert Buzzini, California Farm Bureau RFD, and in San Francisco, I saw Bill Adams at KGO. Bill works out of the same building I originated a western network show on both the Red and Blue some years ago.

　　　　This was an invigorating trip, physically and mentally, and partly because radio farm broadcasting is really in its adult period. The boys over the west that I heard from directly or indirectly on this trip are well organized and know where they are going and what they are doing.

　　　　The AACE elected a strong slate of new officers: Harold Swanson of Minnesota, President; Bill Ward of New York, Vice President; Joe McClelland of Arizona, Secretary-Treasurer; and Bill Calkins of California, Director No. 1. The Association decided to hold the 1954 meeting at Michigan State College.

　　　　　　　　　　　　　　　　　Cordially,

Enclosures:
　Wheat Quota Referendum Leaflet
　Wheat Marketing Quotas Questions
　　and Answers
　The Work of FAO 1951/52
　Garden and Home Food Preser-
　　vation Facts

　　　　　　　　　　　Ken and Don

　　　　　　　　　　　Ken Gapen and Don Looper
　　　　　　　　　　　Radio and Television Service

RFD LETTER
To
Radio Farm Directors
From
Radio and Television Service
Office of Information U. S. Department of Agriculture

U. S. DEPARTMENT OF AGRICULTURE
CURRENT SER/L RECORD
★ AUG 24 1953 ★
U.S. DEPARTMENT OF AGRICULTURE

July 31, 1953
Letter No. 571

Dear Radio Farm Director:

We've been looking this week for a way to communicate to farm broadcasters something of the urgency which we in Washington feel in regard to the wheat quota referendum Friday, August 14. The vote is extremely important -- the time is short -- and it's imperative that farmers understand the issues. We believe we've given you all the facts you can use ... and there's no need to go over them again. But to summarize the Department's <u>attitude</u> toward the wheat marketing quota referendum, here's a message from Secretary Benson:

"Wheat farmers are going to make a very vital decision on Friday, August 14, and the decision is properly theirs alone to make. The Department of Agriculture has gone to great lengths to see that every wheat farmer has had a chance to know exactly what is involved in the referendum. We have tried to present this information in a completely unbiased way. The decision is now up to wheat farmers themselves. We hope that they will all study the situation carefully -- both the supply situation and also what is involved in a quota program -- make their decisions with full understanding of the issues -- and then be sure to vote."

In most counties, there will be several voting places. A farmer can take a half hour off from work and go to the voting place in his work clothes. That's the reason the referendum was set for Friday, the 14th, instead of Saturday, the 15th, the last day the referendum could legally be held. Many farmers go into the county seat on Saturdays, and it was therefore believed that more farmers would be able to participate in a Friday referendum.

At each voting place and in each county the ballots will be counted by a committee of farmers. These will be wired or telephoned to the State PMA offices where State figures will be tabulated and wired or phoned to Washington. It is expected that the preliminary result of the referendum will be announced in Washington on Saturday, the 15th. We hope to have it on the network farm programs that day, unless the vote is so close that the outcome is still in doubt at that time.

State and county PMA offices have been authorized to release to radio and press preliminary reports on the referendum. The complete official national report will likely not be available until about September 1.

Weather Bureau to Expand Agricultural Service

The Weather Bureau has been in touch with us on a plan that we believe will be of great significance to farm broadcasters. The Bureau is going to put greater emphasis on its services to agriculture. It feels that its offices should give more attention to forecasting services geared especially to the needs of farmers in their areas -- that is, to help farmers decide when to cut hay, when to protect fruit trees from frost, when to dry raisins, or whatever decisions are important in a particular farming area.

With this in mind, the Weather Bureau has appointed an agricultural meteorologist for the first time since the Bureau was taken out of the Department of Agriculture in 1940. He is James M. Beall, a graduate of the College of Idaho at Caldwell and Massachusetts Institute of Technology. Mr. Beall is an experienced Bureau employee; he spent 6 years in Alaska for the Bureau, accompanied the Byrd Expedition to the Antarctic in 1947-48, and has spent the last 4 years in Greece working with that Government for the Mutual Security Agency.

Mr. Beall plans to meet with Department of Agriculture officials in a few days to discuss the new plans. He plans to make a trip around the country soon to see for himself what Weather Bureau offices are already doing in the agricultural field. It is recognized that a lot is being done in some areas, but there is lacking an organized country-wide effort. He may be visiting with some of you during this trip.

The new program will involve educating forecasters on the needs of local farmers and coordinating their efforts with those of farm radio, press, county agents, etc. Naturally, the Weather Bureau cannot make operational decisions for farmers. But it wants farmers to have best possible weather information in making their own decisions. We'll keep you informed as the program develops.

Lamb Crop Up for Third Straight Year

The U. S. lamb crop for 1953 is 7 percent above last year -- showing an increase for the third straight year. The lamb crop has increased every year since the record low crop of 1950, and this year brought the biggest rise since that time.

BAE reported this week that the 1953 lamb crop totaled 19,702,000 head, compared with 18,479,000 head raised last year. This year's crop is 10 percent above 1950 but is still 21 percent below the average of the last 10 years. The lamb crop is 8 percent larger than last year in the western states (11 Western, South Dakota and Texas) and 6 percent larger in the Native States.

The percentage lamb crop (that is, the number saved per 100 ewes one year old and over on January 1) is 90.1 this year. It was 88.0 last year and the 10-year average is 86.3.

Yugoslav Impressions of American RFD's

The seven Yugoslav radio editors who were the guests of this Government and the NARFD earlier this year have published an interim report expressing thanks to the Department, the NARFD, the land-grant colleges, and various individuals who worked with them during their study in this country.

It seems to us, from a quick reading of the report, that the Yugoslavs got a great deal of good from their contacts with U.S. farm broadcasters. Some of their translated impressions:

"One of the most important impressions gained on the broadcasts for farmers is that these broadcasts endeavor to give the farmer that which is needed most at the given moment. That means agricultural advice, farm news and most important for American agricultural producers, the situation on the market and weather reports.

"They (RFD's) spend a lot of time in the field and in that way they have the opportunity to find out directly from the farmers what they are most interested in and what they demand mostly from the radio service at the given moment. As far as we are able to notice, the farm radio directors in the United States make use of the great possibilities which the microphone offers. Cooperation between farm radio directors and county agents is continuous and always relates to the most important problems concerning the life and work of farmers and their families.

"The task of the farm radio directors is not an easy one considering the number of broadcasts they have in one day and the variety and length of the broadcasts."

Area Extended for Distress Wheat Loans

The Department announced today the addition of Idaho, Montana, Oregon, and North Dakota to the States in which distress wheat loans will be made to producers under the price support program. Wheat producers in areas or counties designated by PMA State Committees will be able to obtain temporary loans on wheat stored either in temporary facilities or on the ground.

Network Farm and Home Shows August 8

NBC National Farm and Home Hour...Saturday originating at 1:00 to 1:30 p.m. EDT. "USDA Headlines" from Washington. The feature will be an interview with Secretary Benson explaining the wheat marketing quota referendum with Ken Gapen.

ABC American Farmer...Saturday originating at 12:30 to 1:00 p.m. EDT. "Top of the Farm News" from USDA. The feature will be a discussion of plant research in the year ahead with Dr. Albert H. Moseman, Chief of the Bureau of Plant Industry, Soils, and Agricultural Engineering, with Jack Towers.

CBS Radio Farm News...Saturday originating 3:30 to 3:45 p.m. EDT with Claude Mahoney.

Farm Prices Unchanged for Month

Prices received by farmers remained unchanged during the month ending July 15, the BAE said today in its monthly prices report. Livestock and livestock products were up 5 percent, but this was offset by lower prices for most fruit and commercial truck crops.

The index of prices paid rose nearly 1 percent, and as a result the parity ratio (ratio of prices received to prices paid) dropped from 94 for June to 93 for July. There were rises in farm wage rates and in prices of commodities bought by farmers for production, especially feeder livestock.

Flagging to Your Attention

We mailed you Secretary Benson's talk at Milwaukee Thursday and have also briefed it for attachment to this Letter. We also mailed you Assistant Secretary Coke's talk delivered in absentia at the Missouri Balanced Farming Action Day Program Tuesday. Also two talks by Assistant Secretary Davis -- one at East Lansing on Tuesday and one at Cedar Rapids today.

We've also mailed the announcement of a new grain sanitation committee for release Monday, Aug. 3; an announcement of temporary livestock loan committees; and a release assuring dairy farmers in drought area that they are eligible under the emergency feed program.

Congratulations to Kingsbury!

Some of the older RFD's may remember Gil Kingsbury, who used to do an agricultural program every Saturday from Washington for WLW, and did many other Government broadcasts for that station. He's just been elected vice president of the Crosley Broadcasting Corporation.

Cordially,

Ken and Don

Enclosures:
  Beef Recipes
  Loose Housing for Dairy
    Cattle

Ken Gapen and Don Looper
Radio and Television Service

Excerpts from <u>Pointing With Pride</u>, an address by Secretary Benson before the Convention of the American Poultry and Hatchery Federation, Milwaukee, Wis., Thursday, July 30, 1953.

Here in the poultry industry, we have a superb example of what can be accomplished when private individuals work together with government as a team, with the proper objective of scientific advancement and human betterment. This is a case history of what can be accomplished when each of these partners assumes his proper role: the industry doing for itself those things which it can do best and the government doing those things which the industry cannot well do for itself.

Changes made in the industry were made frankly in the hope of profit. There are those who impugn this motive, but let me point out that the consumer today has a superior product at a reasonable price because of the profit-motivated changes you undertook.

The broiler industry has never had price supports. It has encountered its share of rough going, but improved production techniques, modern merchandising methods, and production adjustments which were undertaken voluntarily by the industry, have served to keep it on a fairly even keel.

Turkey producers have had rather extensive government assistance in the last year. However, turkey producers have not been content solely with government aid. On a voluntary basis, they are making a substantial reduction in this year's crop, and I am very pleased to note the vigor with which the turkey industry has embarked on a large and continuing merchandising program.

Let me enumerate some of the difficulties which beset us in agriculture.

Excessive stocks are accumulating for certain commodities whose prices are being supported.

A cost-price squeeze has been pinching the farmers, cutting their prices while costs stay high, shrinking their incomes and raising misgivings about the future.

Drought has struck in the southwest, plunging 300,000 farmers and ranchers and their families into distress.

Cattle prices have declined, bringing severe losses to many farmers and ranchers.

Some of these difficulties are the result of natural causes for which no man can be blamed. The problem of excessive stocks, however, comes from mistakes made in former years. High acreage goals were set and restraints on production were eliminated through the declaring of emergencies. Such a policy was temporarily pleasant for farmers, but it has left us with serious adjustment problems.

Some people have capitalized on these problems and have chosen this time to instill unrest among farmers. Evil days are said to be ahead. It is said that the rug is being pulled out from under the farmers. It is said that we are scuttling farm programs. Of course, this is preposterous. These statements are made by those who stand to gain from such fear mongering, and from those who thoughtlessly repeat what more crafty and subtle people tell them. They do not come from responsible people.

The truth is that net farm income this year, in spite of severe drought, will be about 13.3 billion dollars, which is greater than in 14 of the past 20 years.

With incomes and employment at high levels, customers have an abundant supply of dollars with which to buy food and fiber.

So agriculture is basically sound, despite some trouble spots.

...the remedies available to us in agriculture under present law may not be all that we desire. But they are what we now have. They may not meet our long run objectives. Nevertheless, we shall use every appropriate means available in meeting the problems that beset agriculture. The record indicates that this has been done, and done in good faith. We have been solving inherited problems with inherited tools. Permit me this understatement - it has not been easy.

Meanwhile we have been undertaking a broad review of agricultural programs, with a view toward improvement. This will serve as a basis for our recommendations to the Congress, the policy-making body, charged with the momentous task of providing the best possible agricultural legislation by the end of 1954.

We have not been scuttling farm programs; we have been building them.

I report these things so you will know that the Department of Agriculture is discharging its responsibilities under the law. Further than that, we have used and will continue to use the resources of government in the interest of agriculture whenever prudence advises and the law permits. We will not let the farmers down.